Parachutes Could Carry Us Higher

HIGHER
US
CARRY
COULD
PARACHUTES

Poems About Today

Selected by

Gail Harano Cunningham

Illustrated by

Charles Schorre

♛ Hallmark Editions

HIGHER
US
CARRY
COULD
PARACHUTES

IT'S RAINING IN LOVE
Richard Brautigan

I don't know what it is,
but I distrust myself
when I start to like a girl
       a lot.

It makes me nervous.
I don't say the right things
or perhaps I start
      to examine,
           evaluate,
                compute
      what I am saying.

If I say, "Do you think it's going to rain?"
and she says, "I don't know,"
I start thinking: Does she really like me?

In other words
I get a little creepy.

A friend of mine once said,
"It's twenty times better to be friends
      with someone
than it is to be in love with them."

I think he's right and besides,
it's raining somewhere, programming flowers
and keeping snails happy.
      That's all taken care of.

AMERICAN CITY
Joyce Carol Oates

Only the city's people understand four-thirty.
Afternoon air releases us brazen with
adventure, over the pavement in a flood.
Our muscled legs and leather shoes and our heads
bouncing like crockery—inside the long gassy
horizon we swarm and ask questions. We cannot
be shut up. We are protoplasm.

No disorder here but a rain of soot-flakes
from a policeman's club and a silent stir of
pavement ready to break. The sky does not fall
down on the horns. The clouds do not
yearn downward to this din. Ahead a man in a coat
pauses upon the peak of afternoon, fading with
the fading arc of his cigarette to the street. . . .

The scraps of paper blown by today's wind
drift into shapes of elephants and birds.
The neon lights of restaurants tremble to please.
An Oriental languor to the fumes of cars
and the lowering sun, half a sun, keep us alert:
someone seizes my hand and kisses the fingers,
someone says, "Didn't I see you on television?"

A mad dance rumbles out of darkness
not a subway's cave but the thick twists of pipes
become tunnels. At four-thirty each day in Detroit
the humidity gathers to storm but passes,
pinching our veins ruby-red and our nerves
prickly as darting minnows. Crystal reveals itself
in smashed glass on all eight expressways.

Nothing can pry us out of here, we're wedged.
The city's nervous convulsions crack sidewalks
like the sudden cracks of eggshells. The city's
name drags up muddy visions of car lots and
car heaps, America's gift-toothed dream—
Oh, its name is not Detroit! Unambiguous is
the unnamed city and very alive on the street.
"I met him last week, then on Sunday
we went for a ride. . . . We drove each other crazy."

APOLOGIES

Marge Piercy

Moments
when I care about nothing
except an apple:
red as a mapletree
satin and speckled
tart and winey.

Moments
when body is all:
fast as an elevator
pulsing out waves of darkness
hot as the inner earth
molten and greedy.

Moments
when sky fills my head:
bluer than books
cleaner than number
with a wind
fresh and sour
cold from the mouth of the sea.

Moments
of sinking my teeth
into now like a hungry fox.
Never otherwise
am I so cruel:
never otherwise
so happy.

ABOVE PATE VALLEY

Gary Snyder

We finished clearing the last
Section of trail by noon,
High on the ridge-side
Two thousand feet above the creek—
Reached the pass, went on
Beyond the white pine groves,
Granite shoulders, to a small
Green meadow watered by the snow,
Edged with Aspen—sun
Straight high and blazing
But the air was cool.
Ate a cold fried trout in the
trembling shadows. I spied
A glitter, and found a flake
Black volcanic glass—obsidian—
By a flower. Hands and knees
Pushing the Bear grass, thousands
Of arrowhead leavings over a
Hundred yards. Not one good
Head, just razor flakes
On a hill snowed all but summer,
A land of fat summer deer.
They came to camp. On their
Own trails. I followed my own
Trail here. Picked up the cold-drill,
Pick, singlejack, and sack
Of dynamite.
Ten thousand years.

LAZY PLUMBING

X. J. Kennedy

Letting the water run to get it hot,
I lay back down on my cot
And so did you.

A bobolink
Complained of the loss of water in the sink.

Morning grew hot.
Our coffeepot
Scorched through.

PHOENIX

Helga Sandburg

Before the separation
When the veins of our hands lay often together
And our mouths were understanding
Love-poetry came easy

After our angry voices
I stayed myself from writing
I left arranging of words
Empty windows and dusty doors
Were my world

Now that I have found again the easy sky
And have given up the cough drops
And spring is replacing the cobwebs
That had stretched

I will write another love poem
And give it to
Anyone who passes

FOR A THIRTIETH BIRTHDAY, WITH A BOTTLE OF BURGUNDY

John Hollander

                    Drop by
                    Drop it
                    Empties
                    Now not
                    Even as
                    Our own
                    Tearful
                    Vintage
                    Gathering
                    Itself with
                    Such slowness
                    Gradually might
                    Widen in the bottom
                    Of some oblate vessel
                    But as when the pouring
                    Bottle now nearly half of
                    Its old wine spent delivers
                    The rest up in sobs rapidly
                    Tears years and wine expire
                    As tosspot Time sends after
                    His cellarer once more alas
                    Then let the darkling drops
                    Wept in a decent year along
                    The golden slopes elude for
                    A moment or so his horribly
                    Steady pouring hand and run
                    Into sparkling glasses still
                    Unshattered yes and undimmed

DANIEL AT BREAKFAST
Phyllis McGinley

His paper propped against the electric toaster
 (Nicely adjusted to his morning use),
Daniel at breakfast studies world disaster
 And sips his orange juice.

The words dismay him. Headlines shrilly chatter
 Of famine, storm, death, pestilence, decay.
Daniel is gloomy, reaching for the butter.
 He shudders at the way

War stalks the planet still, and men know hunger,
 Go shelterless, betrayed, may perish soon.
The coffee's weak again. In sudden anger
 Daniel throws down his spoon

And broods a moment on the kitchen faucet
 The plumber mended, but has mended ill;
Recalls tomorrow means a dental visit,
 Laments the grocery bill.

Then, having shifted from his human shoulder
 The universal woe, he drains his cup,
Rebukes the weather (surely turning colder),

 Crumples his napkin up
And, kissing his wife abruptly at the door,
Stamps fiercely off to catch the 8:04.

WAR

Dan Roth

Dawn came slowly,
almost not at all.
The sun crept over the hill
cautiously
fearful of being hit
by mortar fire.

PEACE

Joseph Pintauro

Peace
will
never
happen
until
we can
laugh
at the
stitches
in our
maps
where we
think
we really
split the
planet
into
parts.
. . . until we
share the
land
&
the light
&
the air.

Until we
    mend the
    hearts
        of
men who
  wish to
  breathe
        &
  live,
there
    will
be
        no
peace.

IF ALL THE UNPLAYED PIANOS

Winfield Townley Scott

If all the unplayed pianos in America—
    The antimacassared uprights in old ladies' parlors
    In the storehouses the ones that were rented for
        vaudeville
    The ones where ill fame worsened and finally died
    The ones too old for Sunday School helplessly dusty
    The ones too damp at the beach and too dry in the
        mountains
    The ones mothers used to play on winter evenings
    The ones silenced because of the children growing
        away—
Resounded suddenly all together from coast to coast:
Untuned joy like a fountain jetted everywhere for a
    moment:
The whole nation burst to untapped, untrammeled song:
It would make—in short—a most satisfactory occasion,
A phenomenon which the scientists could never explain.

NIGHTSONG
Philip Booth

Beside you,
lying down at dark,
my waking fits your sleep.

Your turning
flares the slow-banked fire
between our mingled feet,

and there,
curved close and warm
against the nape of love,

held there,
who holds your dreaming
shape, I match my breathing

to your breath;
and sightless, keep my hand
on your heart's breast, keep

nightwatch
on your sleep to prove
there is no dark, nor death.

MUSHROOMS

Sylvia Plath

Overnight, very
Whitely, discreetly,
Very quietly

Our toes, our noses
Take hold on the loam,
Acquire the air.

Nobody sees us,
Stops us, betrays us;
The small grains make room.

Soft fists insist on
Heaving the needles,
The leafy bedding,

Even the paving.
Our hammers, our rams,
Earless and eyeless,

Perfectly voiceless,
Widen the crannies,
Shoulder through holes. We

Diet on water,
On crumbs of shadow,
Bland-mannered, asking

Little or nothing.
So many of us!
So many of us!

We are shelves, we are
Tables, we are meek,
We are edible,

Nudgers and shover
In spite of ourselves.
Our kind multiplies:

We shall by morning
Inherit the earth.
Our foot's in the door.

HOW EVERYTHING HAPPENS

(Based on a study of the Wave)

May Swenson

                                                            happen.
                                                        to
                                                    up
                                            stacking
                                        is
                                    something
When nothing is happening

When it happens
                        something
                                pulls
                                    back
                                        not
                                            to
                                                happen.

    When   has happened.
            pulling back   stacking up
                            happens

        has happened   stacks up.
When it   something   nothing
                                pulls back while

Then nothing is happening.

happens.
                    and
              forward
         pushes
       up
    stacks
 something
Then

CELEBRATING LILIES
Sandra Hochman

I have made love to the yellow lilies,
Turned my face against their cool skin,
Led my lips and eyes to their stamens
While I cried to see anything as bright
As these golden lilies.
How I look for them!

There are people who do not explore the in-
Side of flowers, kissing them,
Resting their own tongues on their petals.
I must tell them. Where will I begin?

And I love
Earth, violently, and vegetables,
Stars, and all things that will not break.
My hair smells of melons, marl, jasmine.

LATE LATE

George Starbuck

Where tomahawks flash in the powwow
and tommyguns deepen the hubbub
and panzers patrol, is the horror
I live without sleep for the love of,

whose A-bombs respond to the tom-tom,
whose halberds react to the ack-ack,
while I, as if slugged with a dumdum,
sit back and sit back and sit back

until the last gunman is drawn on,
last murderous rustler druv loco,
last prisoncamp commandant spat at,
and somehow, and poco a poco,

the bottles are gone from the sixpack,
sensation is gone from the buttocks,
Old Glory dissolves into static,
the box is a box is a box.

APARTMENT HOUSE
Gerald Raftery

A filing-cabinet of human lives
Where people swarm like bees in tunneled hives,
Each to his own cell in the towered comb,
Identical and cramped—we call it home.

A MODERN ROMANCE

Paul Engle

Come live with me and be my wife
And we will lead a packaged life,
Where food, drink, fun, all things save pain
Come neatly wrapped in cellophane.

I am the All-American boy,
Certified as fit for joy,
Elected (best of all the breed)
Hairline most likely to recede.
My parchment scroll to verify
Is stamped in gold and witnessed by
Secretary-Treasurer of
Americans Hundred Per Cent For Love.

You are the All-American girl,
Red toe to artificial curl,
Who passed all tests from skipping rope
And using only Cuddly Soap
To making fire in any weather
By rubbing boy and girl together.

We are the nation's nicest team,
Madison Avenue's magic scheme
To show how boy gets girl: my style
Succeeds by using Denta-Smile.

How merchandised that ceremony!
The minister was scrubbed and bony,
And all was sterile in that room
Except, one hoped, the eager groom.

Married, with advertising's blessing,
We can begin togethernessing.
Before I carry you, my bride,
Across the threshold and inside,
I'll take, to help my milk-fed bones,
Vitamins, minerals and hormones.

Now look how quickly I have fixed
A dry martini (ready-mixed).
So drink to our day, consecrated,
In chairs of leather, simulated.
While you are changing out of those
Nylon, dacron, rayon clothes,
I cook the dinner, without fail
Proving a real American male,
Humble without too much endurance,
But lots of paid-up life insurance.

From the deep-freeze, to please your wish,
A TV dinner in its dish,
All ready-seasoned, heat it up.
Pour instant water in this cup
On instant coffee from a can.
Be proud, love, of your instant man.
Innocent food, mechanized manna
(Except the delicate banana),

Can you endure—forgive the question—
The messy horrors of digestion?

Even our love is pasteurized,
Our gentle hope homogenized.

And now our pure, hygienic night.
To our voluptuous delight
Your hair is up, restraints are down,
And cream is patted on your frown.
The brand-name mattress on the bed
Is wrapped in paper like fresh bread.
We can, to make our own campfire,
Turn the electric blanket higher.
We will cry, Darling, I do care,
In chastely air-conditioned air.

We've read the books, know what to do,
By science, wife, I offer you
This helpful, vacuum-packed, live nerve
(Just add devotion, dear, and serve).
Hurry! Out back I seem to hear
The landlord's Plymouth prowling near.

If this efficient plan produces
By chance (those awful natural juices!)
That product of a thousand uses,
A Junior, wrapped in elastic
Inexpensive bag of plastic
(Just break the seal and throw away)
From antiseptic throats we'll say:
It was an All-American day.

GO BY BROOKS
Leonard Cohen

Go by brooks, love,
Where fish stare,
Go by brooks,
I will pass there.

Go by rivers
Where eels throng,
Rivers, love,
I won't be long.

Go by oceans,
Where whales sail,
Oceans, love,
I will not fail.

I AM A BLACK WOMAN

Mari Evans

I am a black woman
the music of my song
some sweet arpeggio of tears
is written in a minor key
and I
can be heard humming in the night
Can be heard
                humming
in the night

I saw my mate leap screaming to the sea
and I/with these hands/cupped the lifebreath
from my issue in the canebrake
I lost Nat's swinging body in a rain of tears
and heard my son scream all the way from Anzio
for Peace he never knew. . . . I
learned Da Nang and Pork Chop Hill
in anguish
Now my nostrils know the gas
and these trigger tire/d fingers
seek the softness in my warrior's beard

I
am a black woman
tall as a cypress
strong
beyond all definition still
defying place
and time
and circumstance
  assailed
    impervious
      indestructible
Look
  on me and be
renewed

WONDER WANDER

Lenore Kandel

in the afternoon the children walk like ducks
like geese
like from here to there
eyeing bird-trees puppy dogs candy windows
sun balls ice cream wagons
lady bugs rose bushes fenced yards vacant lots
tall buildings
and other things
big business men take big business walks
wear big business clothes
carry big business briefcases   talk about
big business affairs in
big business voices
young girls walk pretty on the streets
stroll the avenues linger by
shop windows   wedding rings   lady hats
shiny dresses   fancy shoes
whisper like turkey hens   passing the time
young men stride on parade   dream headed
wild eyed   eating up the world
with deep glances   rubbing empty fingers
in their empty pockets and
planning

me, I wander around soft-shoed   easy-legged
watching the scene as it goes
finding things   sea-gull feathers   pink baby roses
every time I see a letter on the sidewalk
I stop and look   it might be
                    for me

STEAM SHOVEL
Charles Malam

The dinosaurs are not all dead.
   I saw one raise its iron head
To watch me walking down the road
Beyond our house today.
Its jaws were dripping with a load
Of earth and grass that it had cropped.
It must have heard me where I stopped,
Snorted white steam my way,
And stretched its long neck out to see,
And chewed, and grinned quite amiably!

TO BE IN LOVE
Gwendolyn Brooks

           To be in love
Is to touch things with a lighter hand.

In yourself you stretch, you are well.

You look at things
Through his eyes.
        A Cardinal is red.
        A sky is blue.
Suddenly you know he knows too.
He is not there but
You know you are tasting together
The winter, or light spring weather.

His hand to take your hand is overmuch.
Too much to bear.

THE CREATURES OF THE ZODIAC

Margaret Atwood

In the daytime I am brave,
I draw my gloves on finger
by finger, my money
behaves itself in my purse
the food rolls over on my plate
there are no omens

I have everything under control

But at night the constellations
emerge; I clench
my feet to boots
my face to a wire mask

Their whitehard eyes bristle
behind the bars, their teeth
grow larger for being starved

They were once dust and ordinary
hatreds. I breathed on them, named them:
now they are predictions.

COME LIE
        WITH ME
AND BE
        MY LOVE
Lawrence Ferlinghetti

Come lie with me and be my love
Love lie with me
Lie down with me
Under the cypress tree
In the sweet grasses
Where the wind lieth
Where the wind dieth
As night passes
Come lie with me
All night with me
And have enough of kissing me
And have enough of making love
And let my lizard speak to thee
And let our two selves speak
All night under the cypress tree
Without making love

THE ABORTION

Anne Sexton

Somebody who should have been born
is gone.

Just as the earth puckered its mouth,
each bud puffing out from its knot,
I changed my shoes, and then drove south.

Up past the Blue Mountains, where
Pennsylvania humps on endlessly,
wearing, like a crayoned cat, its green hair,

its roads sunken in like a gray washboard;
where, in truth, the ground cracks evilly,
a dark socket from which the coal has poured,

Somebody who should have been born
is gone.

the grass as bristly and stout as chives,
and me wondering when the ground would break,
and me wondering how anything fragile survives;

up in Pennsylvania, I met a little man,
not Rumpelstiltskin, at all, at all . . .
he took the fullness that love began.

Returning north, even the sky grew thin
like a high window looking nowhere.
The road was as flat as a sheet of tin.

Somebody who should have been born
is gone.

Yes, woman, such logic will lead
to loss without death. Or say what you meant,
you coward . . . this baby that I bleed.

AT THE AIRPORT
Howard Nemerov

Through the gate, where nowhere and night begin,
A hundred suddenly appear and lose
Themselves in the hot and crowded waiting room.
A hundred other herd up toward the gate,
Patiently waiting that the way be opened
To nowhere and night, while a voice recites
The intermittent litany of numbers
And the holy names of distant destinations.

None going out can be certain of getting there.
None getting there can be certain of being loved
Enough. But they are sealed in the silver tube
And lifted up to be fed and cosseted,
While their upholstered cell of warmth and light
Shatters the darkness, neither here nor there.

'KEEPSAKES'
William Stafford

STAR GUIDES:
   Any star is enough
   if you know what star it is.

KIDS:
   They dance before they learn
   there is anything that isn't music.

THE LIMBS OF THE PIN OAK TREE:
   "Gravity—what's that?"

AN ARGUMENT AGAINST
THE EMPIRICAL METHOD:
   Some haystacks don't even have any needle.

COMFORT:
   We think it is calm here,
   or that our storm is the right size.

AMBITION

Morris Bishop

I got pocketed behind 7X-3824;
He was making 65, but I can do a little more.
I crowded him on the curves, but I couldn't get past,
And on the straightaways there was always some truck
      coming fast.
Then we got to the top of a mile-long incline   ·
And I edged her out to the left, a little over the white line,
And ahead was a long grade with construction at the
      bottom,

And I said to the wife, "Now by golly I got'm!"
I bet I did 85 going down the long grade,
And I braked her down hard in front of the barricade,
And I swung in ahead of him and landed fine
Behind 9W-7679.

HOW TO EAT A POEM
Eve Merriam

Don't be polite.
Bite in.
Pick it up with your fingers and lick the juice that
    may run down your chin.
It is ready and ripe now, whenever you are.

You do not need a knife or fork or spoon
or plate or napkin or tablecloth.

For there is no core
or stem
or rind
or pit
or seed
or skin
to throw away.

PARACHUTES, MY LOVE,
COULD CARRY US HIGHER

Barbara Guest

I just said I didn't know
And now you are holding me
In your arms,
How kind.
Parachutes, my love, could carry us higher.
Yet around the net I am floating
Pink and pale blue fish are caught in it,
They are beautiful,
But they are not good for eating.
Parachutes, my love, could carry us higher
Than this mid-air in which we tremble,
Having exercised our arms in swimming,
Now the suspension, you say,
Is exquisite, I do not know.
There is coral below the surface,
There is sand, and berries
Like pomegranates grow,
This wide net, I am treading water
Near it, bubbles are rising and salt
Drying on my lashes, yet I am no nearer
Air than water. I am closer to you
Than land and I am in a stranger ocean
Than I wished.

D.O.M., A.D. 2167

John Frederick Nims

When I've outlived three plastic hearts, or four,
Another's kidneys, corneas *(beep!),* with more
Unmentionable rubber, nylon, such—
And when *(beep!)* in a steel drawer (DO NOT TOUCH!),
Mere brain cells in a saline wash, I thrive
With thousands, taped to quaver out, "Alive!"—
God grant that steel two wee *(beep!)* eyes of glass
To glitter wicked when the nurses pass.

CUPID'S GRIN
Michael McClure

Yes! This damn universe!
An ever-flowing, eternal, closed up,
open system—a dial of vibratory flows
from end to front—a technicolor timeless object—
Stars—stars—nebulae—and swirls
of growing energy that fantasizes self.
A living statue of a song!
(Amoeba daydreams Metazoa.
Helium imagines Milky Way!
Or start from either end.)
Alive as the sea!
When it all begins
I'll be there.
You'll know me by my curling lips

—And chuckle

A TUNE FOR THE TELETYPE
William Jay Smith

O Teletype, tell us of time clocks and trouble,
Wheels within wheels, rings within rings;
In each little ring a pretty wire basket,
In each pretty basket any number of things—

Things to be stamped and dispatched in good order:
O tell us of code clerks and typists who toil
So the world may receive the good news in the morning,
And H-bombs explode according to Hoyle!

H-bombs explode and each pretty wire basket
With bits of charred paper fly off through the air!
The question is answered, but who's there to ask it?
The man with the question is no longer there.

The question-man now is somewhere in orbit;
He's calling—click-click—the whole human race.
A man in the moon, but no cow to jump over—
End of the poem . . . Space . . . Space . . . Space . . . Space . . .

BEDTIME

Denise Levertov

We are a meadow where the bees hum,
mind and body are almost one

as the fire snaps in the stove
and our eyes close,

and mouth to mouth, the covers
pulled over our shoulders,

we drowse as horses drowse afield,
in accord; though the fall cold

surrounds our warm bed, and though
by day we are singular and often lonely.

SONIC BOOM
John Updike

I'm sitting in the living room,
When, up above, the Thump of Doom
Resounds. Relax. It's sonic boom.

The ceiling shudders at the clap,
The mirrors tilt, the rafters snap,
And Baby wakens from his nap.

"Hush, babe. Some pilot we equip,
Giving the speed of sound the slip,
Has cracked the air like a penny whip."

Our world is far from frightening; I
No longer strain to read the sky
Where moving fingers (jet planes) fly.
Our world seems much too tame to die.

And if it does, with one more pop,
I shan't look up to see it drop.

BALL-POINT, FAREWELL
Norman Rosten

They are giving away ball-point pens again,
Although it is clear the game is up.
The ball-point began as a hot item
Replacing the leaky pen-point for awhile:
It wrote through butter but failed at cheese.
Then the humidity caused it to falter.
Or tiny fungi on the page stopped it cold.
Justice will not be denied the pen world:
The point-pen started a grim comeback,
Its graph hot on the ball-line, finally
Crossing it with a great leap of ink.
The ball-point began a massive counterattack:
All the sagacity and tensile wit of Avenue
Madison with various gimmicks free cartridges
Different ball sizes and intensities including
Replaceable and interchangeable balls
Until the situation we have today;
They are giving 'em away.
They are dropping 'em from buildings,
They are popping out of bank books, coffins,
And cereal boxes, scattered to all takers
Especially newlyweds—free, free, free!

(And the rumor that an old model,
Pre-plastic but in good condition,
Was forced on a tourist at gun point,
In broad daylight, outside Radio City Music Hall)

FOURTEEN
Rod McKuen

How can we be sure of anything
                    the tide changes.
The wind that made the grain wave gently yesterday
        blows down the trees of tomorrow.
And the sea sends sailors crashing on the rocks,
as easily as it guides them safely home.
                    I love the sea
but it doesn't make me less afraid of it
                    I love you
but I'm not always sure of what you are
and how you feel.

THE QUAKE
Lucien Stryk

Alone in that paper house
We laughed when the bed
Heaved twice then threw
Us to the floor. When all

Was calm again, you said
It took an earthquake
To untwine us. Then I
Stopped your shaking

With my mouth. Together
In this place of brick,
Held firm as fruits
Upon a sculptured bough,

Our loving is more safe.
Then why should dream
Return us to that fragile
Shelf of land? And why,

Our bodies twined upon
This couch of stone,
Should we be listening,
Like dead sinners, for the quake?

(UNTITLED)
Lucille Clifton

in the inner city
or
like we call it
home
we think a lot about uptown
and the silent nights
and the houses straight as
dead men
and the pastel lights
and we hang on to our no place
happy to be alive
and in the inner city
or like we call it
home

EACH MORNING
(SECTION 4 FROM
"HYMN FOR LANIE POO")

LeRoi Jones

Each morning
I go down
to Gansevoort St.
and stand on the docks.
I stare out
at the horizon
until it gets up
and comes to embrace
me. I
make believe
it is my father.
This is known
as genealogy.

POEM TO BE READ AT 3 A.M.
Donald Justice

Excepting the diner
On the outskirts
The town of Ladora
At 3 A.M.
Was dark but
For my headlights
And up in
One second-story room
A single light
Where someone
Was sick or
Perhaps reading
As I drove past
At seventy
Not thinking
This poem
Is for whoever
Had the light on.

INDEX

Composed in Optima, a Roman face
of graceful simplicity
designed by Hermann Zapf.
Printed on Hallmark Eggshell Book paper.
Set at The Castle Press,
Grant Dahlstrom, Proprietor.
Designed by Marjorie Merena.